BIG MOUTH
BIG DREAMS

Your Guide to Speaking BIG Dreams Into Existence

Daniela Gabrielle

ALSO BY DANIELA GABRIELLE

Fly Free: Finding the Courage to Live Without Limitations

Inaugurate Your Life: Creating A Roadmap To Change

Expand My Life: 90-Day Life Organization System

motique media

Publishing division of Motique Momentums, LLC

www.danielaGabrielle.com

Copyright © 2014 Daniela Gabrielle Smallwood

All rights reserved.

ISBN:069220265X
ISBN-13:9780692202654

DEDICATION

This is book is dedicated to all of the **DREAMERS** and **GOAL-GETTERS** who were told to get their heads out of the clouds and simply be ordinary. May this book break every ounce of mediocrity in your heart, mind and body. There's a **BIG** dream inside of you and it's time to bring it forth.

Let's Put Our
BIG Dreams
In Motion
With Our Words!

I Love You To Life,

Daniela Gabrielle

DANIELA GABRIELLE

PART I
EIGHT LIFE LESSONS FOR BIG MOUTHS & BIG DREAMERS

LESSON ONE
There's Nothing Wrong With Your BIG Dream

LESSON TWO
Before You Can Transform Your Conversation,
You Must Transform Your Heart

LESSON THREE
Your Mouth Is A Lethal Weapon

LESSON FOUR
Send Your Words In the Direction You Want Your Life To Go

LESSON FIVE
Don't Just Talk About It, Be About It

LESSON SIX
Say What You Want and Want What You Say

LESSON SEVEN
It Is What It Is, Correction, It Is What I Declare

LESSON EIGHT
You Are Destined For The Finish

PART II
THE DREAMER'S CHARGE

PART III
21- Days of Big Mouthed Dream Activation

INTRODUCTION

Growing up as a child my mouth got me in more trouble than I could ever imagine. Report cards from kindergarten to high school always so eloquently reported, "Talks too much!" Report card in and out, marking period after marketing period, year after year this mouth got me in trouble. Well, I guess it REALLY wasn't the report card's fault, but that mouth of mine definitely took me places I did not want to be. It didn't end there, I didn't just talk too much I was also very loud. My mom called it, "Loud for no good reason!"

My voice could reverberate a room like nobody's business. I didn't need a microphone, I had a built in microphone for a voice. You could hear me before you saw me. That mouth of mine was causing me lots of trouble. It made people uncomfortable. Everyone around me made it their mission to make me to tone me down, shut up, and whatever I did, **"STOP TALKING!"** No one told me how powerful this mouth of mine was, and that if I tapped into my life's purpose, that this ole' big mouth could call forth a world of change in my life and in the lives of those around me.

Often times, the very thing we are called to do, is the very thing that we come under attack for. We find ourselves victims of statutory rape, as the enemy steps in during the most vulnerable times of our lives. It's designed to kill our confidence and sow seeds of doubt. It took years for me to come into the knowledge that my mouth was the vehicle that God would use to carry out my purpose here on earth. I had to break past every remnant of old. From the whispers of my past that told me I was too loud, too wordy, too over the top, and too much to be accepted. I had to break free.

It has been the foolish things that the world laughed at and mocked that God has used to confound the wise. Those areas that seemed wasted and empty, God strengthened and released to the world through me. I always carried the dream that I would speak on platforms across the world; that my voice would be heard on television, radio, and through multimedia outlets.

That very thing the devil tried to kill has been the thing that has ushered me into new dimensions of possibility and brought prosperity to my life.

Think back, where have you found the most pressure to abandon your gifts? What's the thing inside of you that others tried to squash, contain, shutdown or push out? Somewhere in all of that adversity, lies a dream and a vision from God to carry out a purpose that adds value to the world around you.

It is my prayer that as you read this book, that you will connect with those BIG dreams that reside within you. I pray that my BIG mouth will inspire you to open up and speak to the dream in your life until you see it come to past.

There was no one around to cultivate my big mouth and loud voice growing up. I went through a long season resenting the gift that God gave me. When I came into the knowledge of how a BIG mouth can unlock everything I need to fulfill my assignment on the earth, I was able to enter into places I never imagined.

Let's take a journey into a world where money doesn't matter, your degrees hold little validity, your credentials are not important and who you know does not determine where you go. This is the place where you boldly allow your mouth to make way for your BIG dream.

Learn to declare and decree over your future using spiritual principles that will transform your life and pave the way towards your dream.

I've broken the content of this book into three parts. Part I lays a foundation for why BIG dreamers need to have BIG mouths. It teaches you how to transform your mouth into a lethal weapon that makes room from for your ever-expanding life using the life lessons I've experienced living my BIG dream. You'll dig into truths that help you build the confidence necessary to speak into your future.

Part II is my personal charge for you to activate your BIG mouth and BIG dream. This is where you'll be stirred to action and inspired to ditch a mediocre life.

Part III is for activation. Here you will find declarations, decrees, confessions, and affirmations that you can use daily in your own 21-day Big Mouthed Dreamer journey. Your mouth is a powerful weapon. Use it for good. Use it for purpose. Use it to talk your way right into your BIG DREAMS!

FREQUENTLY USED VOCABULARY

Affirmation- a statement is declared to be true

To the praise of the glory of his grace, wherein he hath made us accepted in the beloved - Ephesians 1:6

Declaration- A formal statement or decree

I shall not die, but live, and declare the works of the Lord. –Psalms 118:17

Confession- a formal profession of a believe

Whosoever therefore shall confess me before men, him will I confess also before my Father which is in heaven. –Matthew 10:32

Decree- a formal and authorities order

Thou shalt also decree a thing, and it shall be established unto thee: and the light shall shine upon thy ways.

–Job 22:28

Part I

The Lessons That Transformed my BIG Mouth
and BIG Dream

Lesson 1

There's Nothing Wrong With Your BIG Dream

"The future belongs to those who believe in the beauty of their dreams."

Eleanor Roosevelt

One of the coolest things about being a child was the innocent faith that that made us invincible, uninhibited and free. We had imagination for days and there was absolutely nothing that could stop our creativity. Somewhere along the path of life we lost that. We lost the art of not only dreaming, but also believing that our dreams could come true. If we can return to that place of faith in God and in ourselves, we can lead our lives with greater passion and fulfillment.

Go to school, get a college degree, get a job, get married and have a kid or two, buy a house with a white picket fence, retire, and die. That's the cycle of redundancy and normalcy that most people aim for in life. While some call it the American Dream, I call it my worst nightmare.

The world calls being realistic and having security, stability. I call it boring and ordinary. Around the globe it has become commonplace to be "normal". When I was in the military there was a saying that said, "Shut up and color." So many people have settled to do just that. We color in the lines, stay in our rightful place and go through life unseen and unheard.

We've learned to think inside of the box and to fit to society's measure stick of success. What happens when you have a BIG dream that just won't keep silent? What do you do when your BIG dreams keep you awake at night and beckon you to something greater than what you're doing right now? How do you continue to ignore your call to live and fulfill your BIG dream?

You don't.

READY. AIM. FIRE.

Say this out loud right now, ***"There's nothing wrong with my BIG dream!"***

It's time to get out of your own head and evict the squatters that hang out in your mind keeping you from pursuing that BIG vision down on the inside of you. No more using others as your measurement of success. It's time for you to develop your own roadmap and become accountable for the vision that God has given you for your life.

Earlier as you were reading I had you stop, drop and declare that there's nothing wrong with your BIG dream. Many of times we aren't moving forward with our BIG dream because we have convinced ourselves that our dream is impossible. If you are going to get to the other side of your BIG dream, it's important to transform your heart by opening up your life to what is possible.

Don't be moved by what others think is right or wrong for your life any longer. It's time for you to get truthful with yourself about what you really desire for your life.

Before you can be convinced that your BIG dream is possible, it's vital that you identify what your BIG dream actually is and tap into why you are not pursuing it.

What's Your BIG Dream?

Take a few moments to write or draw out your BIG dream in the space provided.

_____
_____
_____
_____
_____
_____

Why haven't you pursued your BIG dream?

Don't skip over this part, it's important to identify where your hesitation is coming from if you're going to truly move towards your BIG dream.

_____
_____
_____
_____
_____
_____

Common Reasons People Don't Pursue Their BIG Dreams

- ✓ Fear of failure
- ✓ Fear of success
- ✓ Fear of what will others say
- ✓ Lack of resources
- ✓ Lack of know-how

There are millions of reasons that you can find to not pursue you BIG dream, however the time and energy that you spend making excuses could be productive time and energy spent fueling your faith and getting into action.

Channel Your **BIG** Dream Inspiration

Think about all of the people you know that had a BIG dream and were bold enough to do it. Oprah, Dr. Martin Luther King Jr, Tyler Perry, Donald Trump, Kimora Lee Simmons, Kandi Burruss, Bishop T.D. Jakes, Joel Osteen and others were all ordinary people with extraordinary dreams who ignored their critics and went on to lead lives others only dream of.

Who are your biggest inspirations? Write them down and remind yourself that if it can happen for them, "it can happen for me."

My Big Dream Inspiration #1

_____

My Big Dream Inspiration #2

_____

My Big Dream Inspiration #1

_____

Before You Can Transform Your Conversation, You Must Transform Your Heart

> "We are masters of the unsaid words, but slaves of those we let slip out."
>
> Winston Churchill

One of my favorite places for inspiration in my personal and professional life lie within the two covers of the Holy Bible. I use it as a guide for strength, courage, and wisdom as I wildly chase a dream that others can't understand. It helps me build a vision that will outlast my life on Earth. Before we can dive into changing our conversation and our confessions, we must start with our heart.

One of my favorite principles in regards to speaking BIG dreams into existence is based in these three scriptures:

For as he thinketh in his heart, so is he...

Proverbs 23:7

Keep thy heart with all diligence; for out of it are the issues of life.

Proverbs 4:23

... For of the abundance of the heart his mouth speaketh

Luke 6:45

Through these passages of scripture we find that what we think about ourselves, is what is so in our lives. If we don't think that our BIG dream is possible, our actions and conversation begin to align with our words. Think about how many times you've talked yourself out of something, not because you couldn't do it, but because you didn't believe you could accomplish it.

As we look at these three scriptures you'll see that there is a chain reaction that takes place on the inside long before words ever begin to leave your mouth. Let's start from conversation and work our way backwards.

... For of the abundance of the heart his mouth speaketh

Luke 6:45

What is our heart?

Our heart is the **seat of our emotions** and as Proverbs 4:23 reveals it is where we house the issues of life. All of the issues that we experience hang out in our heart and if we haven't explored our hearts and dealt with certain issues they become seeds that bloom and flow out in our conversation.

Keep thy heart with all diligence; for out of it are the issues of life.

Proverbs 4:23

Have you ever been talking and just blurted out something and you had no clue where it came from?

I like to call it **word vomit.** It's when the issues on the inside become stirred for one reason or another and usually unaware to the speaker, words just fall out of our mouths. Many times we walk through life speaking what is in our hearts based on the good and the bad experiences we have encountered in our lives. These experiences shape our conversation as well as our thoughts.

For as he thinketh in his heart, so is he...

Proverbs 23:7

If you are going to get up and start moving towards your BIG dream, it's important that you pay attention to your conversation. Your current conversation will reveal issues that are holding you back, keeping you held hostage with fear and doubt and have self-sabotaged your dream thus far.

If you want to know what you'll look like in ten years, listen to what you are saying about your life. I can remember a season in my life where I was desperately stuck in a rut. Deep down I knew that where I was geographically and emotionally was not the best launching pad for my BIG dream, however I would not pull the trigger on making a move. I spent three years convincing myself that it was my calling to live in a place that made me miserable doing something I was no longer happy to do.

When challenged about my current situation, I would say, "I'm just meant to be in the background. This is where I am meant to be." The truth was that I wasn't meant to be in the background. That wasn't my BIG dream and it wasn't God's desire for my heart, but it was the level of faith I had in my own ability to do something extraordinary in my life.

It would be easy for me to just give you a handbook full of positive words that you could read out loud to transform your life. Although helpful, until you pull up those self-sabotaging lies in your heart, you'll always revert back to negative conversation.

Freedom to live a BIG dream and speak inspired words of hope and faith come from letting go. Learning to let go of hurt, disappointment, past failures and the opinions of others that cloud your heart and pollute your conversation can change your life.

Breaking Free to Dream BIG

I have some family members that I love with all of my heart, but it breaks my heart to be in their presence because every word that comes out of their mouths is negative. When I come around them I need a giant sized shield just to protect myself from the spewing negativity. For years this made me believe that they were negative people who didn't love me or believe in me. I used to allow them to get in my head, destroy my confidence, and talk me out of the very things that were calling me towards my BIG dream.

It wasn't until I came into the knowledge of these three scriptures that I understood that negative people aren't bad people, they are hurting people leading their lives from a place of insecurity, fear and disappointment. Their negative words aren't a reflection of who I am as a person, they're a reflection of who they believe themselves to be.

You can't change another person's reflection of themselves, but you definitely don't have to accept their truth as your own. Start rejecting other people's projections onto your life and dreams. Cleanse your heart.

READY. AIM. FIRE.
Say this out loud right now, ***"I am not what they say I am. I won't do what they said I'd do. I won't be what they declared I'd be. I am who God created me to be and walking out my BIG dream is part of my destiny!"***

As a BIG mouth person, with a BIG dream, getting to the other side of your dream starts with a cleansing of the heart. It's time to release those things that keep your conversation muddy, unproductive and self-deprecating. Dig deep into the things you say that are holding you back today. Choose to let them go and eradicate them from your vocabulary.

Start With You

What conversations are coming out of your mouths that don't serve your BIG dreams?

_____
_____
_____
_____
_____
_____
_____
_____
_____
_____
_____
_____
_____
_____

BIG MOUTH BIG DREAMS

DANIELA GABRIELLE

What does a life of letting go look like for you?

Take a few moments to write or draw out your vision of a life free from other people's negative words in the space provided.

The BIG Release

Letting go starts today. Think about the issues and hurtful things that have happened to you and been said to you that have formed negative thoughts about your life. In the space provided, write a letter letting go, forgiving, and moving forward. After you write it, read it aloud daily until you feel you have whole-heartedly released it from your life.

Dear God,

Over the years I have grown to believe *(Insert those self-sabotaging beliefs that pollute your conversation.)*

_____
_____
_____
_____. These thoughts entered my life when *(Talk about the issues that created this belief.)* _____

_____
_____
_____.

Believing these negative lies about my life has kept me from *(Insert the impact of believing these lies. Consider how they've affected how you see and speak about yourself)* _____ _____ _____ _____ _____. Today I choose to let go of these beliefs and to detach myself from this self-fulfilling prophecy.

I forgive _____ for every negative impartation that has brought parts of my life to a stand still. I recognize that they themselves are hurting and I no longer hold them accountable for my destiny. I release them from every debt I've held them to and I no longer need their acceptance to embrace my BIG dream. I forgive myself for every negative, un-productive word of death that has come from my mouth. Wash over my heart with healing and purify my words with purpose.

BIG MOUTH BIG DREAMS

I choose to agree with God that my BIG dream to

_____

_____

_____ is possible. As I let go of issues that have hurt me, I declare that my heart is transforming my conversation into fierce bold life-giving conversation that will attract what I need to succeed. I lack in nothing and I step into everything that was meant for my life.

Today is a new day. Old things have passed away and my life is made new. This is my new season and my life will never be the same.

It is so!

Love,

_____

Lesson 3

Your Mouth Is A Lethal Weapon

> *"We have two ears and one mouth so that we can listen twice as much as we speak."*
>
> Epictetus

This is a quote commonly used in communication and relationship courses to express the need for people to be good listeners in conversations. In our society there is such a large push to be quiet. We are uncomfortable around talkers. We shy away from loud mouths. We hold our tongues about the things that matter most to us. We've all felt it, that overwhelming feeling to shut up and keep our thoughts to ourselves. People have idly talked recklessly for so long that the mouth now has a bad reputation.

Conversation that stretches our faith, stirs creativity, unlocks purpose and challenges the status quo has been replaced with shallow and senseless small talk. We are afraid to truly speak from our hearts. Think about it, how many times have you chosen not to share your dream or speak about what is important to you out of fear?

People say, "be careful who you tell your dream to because the world is full of dream stealers who will destroy your dream." Here's the truth. No one can steal you BIG dream unless you allow them to. Your BIG dream is your assignment and legacy in the earth. You have a right to believe that your BIG dream is possible. You have a right to pursue that BIG dream with all diligence. You have a right to share and express what's most important to you. Most of all you have a right to not let other's opinion about you or your BIG dream keep you quiet.

One of my favorite movies growing up was Dirty Dancing *(judge me if you may, but it was the Dancing With the Stars of my time).* I can remember rewinding the VHS tape back over and over again to learn the finale dance to "I Had The Time of My Life" by Billy Medley and Jennifer Warnes. If you've never seen it, look it up on YouTube. It's too cute!

I loved that dance, because the choreography wouldn't let me sit still. Beyond the choreography, I loved message that entire scene conveyed. The Dirty Dancing finale gave a quiet shy girl with a talent she didn't even know she had, the opportunity to shine.

The main character Baby was a shy daddy's girl who became friends with the bad boy dance instructor Johnny at the resort where Baby's family was vacationing. She was forbidden to see the new friend she'd met any longer because her father didn't approve. Her father shut down her friendship, love and dancing that was unlocked by being around him and his friends.

In the last scene, Johnny returns to the resort for the finale event to find Baby shoved in the corner seemingly quiet, broken and discouraged. It is here that Johnny played by Patrick Swayze delivered one of the most iconic lines of the movie,

"Nobody puts Baby in the corner."

How many times have you been put in the corner? How many times have you sent your BIG dream to "time out" because you felt incapable of achieving your goal? How many times have you held back your opinion and ran away from the spotlight because you were told that you incapable of doing something?

I've come to be your Johnny. I'm dragging you, your gifts, talents, abilities and BIG dreams out of the corner! Today it's time to let your BIG dream be heard and seen. Take center stage on the platform of life and shine like you've never shined before.

Let your conversation flow. Be bold and speak life. Don't allow your voice to be silenced another moment. You were created to yield your words like the powerful weapon they are.

READY. AIM. FIRE.

Say this out loud right now, **"Nobody puts _____ (insert your name) in a corner!"**

Although listening is a needed and necessary skill, I want to challenge your thinking. I'm ready to redeem the mouth's reputation in your life. I want to help you harness your words so that you can achieve success and fulfillment on a day-to-day basis.

Yes we all have two ears. We have two small ear canals, however the mouth in size is three to four times larger. Listening is vital but speaking is transformative.

The reason that there is such an emphasis on listening is because the average person does not consider the power of their conversation. Reaching back to my favorite life roadmap, the Bible shares with us that the power of life and death are in our tongue (Proverbs 8:21).

We have the capability to use our words to create the world around us. The things that we want to live are brought to life with our words and what we want to die can be put to death with our words. The problem is that we have not considered the depth and breadth of our conversation.

Your mouth is the key to unlocking your BIG dream. As a lethal weapon, you have the authority to speak up and turn down the words around you. Stop being afraid of other people's response to your conversation. Just as they have a right to their opinion, you have the right, authority and power to not receive their negative criticism in your life.

If you've ever hung out with church people for any length of time, especially charismatic church folk I'm sure you've heard this a time or two in your life, "I don't receive that!" It's something often said in response to a comment that is negative or that they don't want to come to fruition in their lives. As silly it may be to some, it is one of the most profound and powerful bullets shot out of a person's mouth. In those four little words, they've just annihilated someone else's power over their life.

Be bold enough to speak up about the things in your world that are important to you. Those who are uplifted, inspired or empowered by your confident conversation would amaze you. You have no clue how critical your conversation is to the world around you. Let your conversations be life giving. When faced with opposition, transform your mouth into a lethal weapon and simply declare, "I don't receive that!"

Your BIG Dream Ammunition

A modern shoot down to negativity in your life comes from one of my favorite artists, Tamar Braxton. She is known for a good line and this one will take out a hater and block what people call "shade" *(shade is when someone delivers a low blow in a nice nasty way)* in your life. When you say something she doesn't agree with or believe to hold true in her life, she'll look at them and say, "You tried it!" Yes, for those of us that love a good Tay-Tay line, this is cute, but listen to what she really said.

YOU – TRIED - IT!

What does that really mean? It means someone attempted to release his or her opinion of your life into your life and it did not work. Remember what we discussed previously, our own issues and state of heart drive our conversation. Therefore someone's opinion of us is often, not always, but often a true reflection of their own thoughts regarding their own lives. Return to sender. You really tried it.

Here's another funny and creative shoot down. Now this one isn't quite as tactful but it gets the job done. This classic line is from the 1990's hit show, Martin. If you said the wrong thing in this comedian's presence you were bound to hear this famous line, "Get to Steppin'!" He would drag that last syllable of stepping out and then give you what we called "the hand." Yes, it's a little out there but the concept is the same. We have a right and responsibility to guard what we allow to take root in our lives.

Now it's your turn!

Let's get creative with our negativity shoot downs. You don't have to be rude, ugly or ignorant when responding to words that come to destroy your BIG dreams. You just have to confidently reject those words before they take power in your life. "I don't receive that" may not be the most appropriate response, depending on the environment.

Create three of your own "go-to" statements

that you can use to politely but firmly shoot down the dream stealers and faith robbers you encounter. Make it fit your style and personality. Have fun.

This is your shooting range...ready, aim and fire!

1) _____

2) _____

3) _____

BIG MOUTH BIG DREAMS

Lesson 4

Send Your Words In the Direction You Want Your Life To Go

> "The best way to predict your future is to create it."
>
> Abraham Lincoln

If you want to know exactly where your life will be in ten years look at what you are saying today. You words hold creative power and they shape the world around you. When God created the world, he didn't think about it. It wasn't some good idea in His head that He just wished to come true. He stood boldly and declared, "Let there be" and there was. If you are created in God's image, you are created in His likeness and the same creative power that He used to speak the world into existence is accessible in your own life.

The problem is that we allow our conversation to be dictated by our "right now" reality instead of using our words to exercise our faith and shape our future. What we talk about is what we hear and what we hear reinforced over time, is what we become. Have you ever seen someone that was really beautiful, but yet they felt or carried themself as if they were ugly, unworthy, and unlovable? The reason they believe that is because of what they have heard reinforced over and over again.

It doesn't take long to believe a reinforced message. First, you hear it. After awhile you begin saying it to yourself. Next thing you know you're saying it out loud. From there it grows into believing it. Before you know it, your actions have fully aligned to a self-sabotaging belief and your life moves in the direction of that self-fulfilling prophecy.

As a child, I got ahold of a very deadly and self-sabotaging song. It was a song I heard a girl sing when I went to the babysitters' house and it went like this,

"Nobody likes me, everybody hates me, I even hate myself."

There were no other lyrics to this song, just these three death penalty statements. I picked up that tune and sang day after day for years. I started singing this song when I was somewhere between the ages of five or six and by the time I reached a teenager, I was convinced that life wasn't worth living. I battled with suicidal thoughts throughout my teens and early twenties. I attempted to take my life with pills and cutting. Once I even tried to drive myself off of the side of the road.

Those words took root in my life. The issues of low esteem and hopelessness flowed out of my heart, through my mouth, and back into my ears on a regular basis. I could feel the pain of that dreadful song everyday. I believed those words. I believed that I was unloved and unworthy to live. I walked out my life from the lens of that lie.

It wasn't until years later that I discovered the root of my self-rejection stemmed from what seemed like a silly schoolyard song. If I was going to turn my life around, I had to start by turning my words around.

These were what I call dysfunctional directional decrees. They are the declarations that people make about their lives that hinder their ability to function at their optimal potential. They get in the way of purpose and keep people from pursuing those BIG dreams.

The first thing I needed to do was disarm the negative words in my life. I started by acknowledging the declarations I made about myself that led me to malfunction in my purpose. It wasn't easy to face my words, but I had to in order to embrace the positive direction I wanted my life to go in.

You may be saying, Daniela Gabrielle, I didn't get this book to look into my past, I wanted this book to learn how to speak into my future. This is what I say to you; your future will contend with what you don't face.

It would be such a shame to get to the place you've been dreaming about for years and then your issues from the past pop up to contend with the success of your future.

No, you may not be able to deal with everything at one time, but as you create a limitless life with your words you want to disconnect from the limiting words of old.

Come out of agreement with the lies and dysfunction that you've spoken over your life. Replace them with new declarations that stir and excite your new life.

READY. AIM. FIRE.

Say this out loud right now,

"I denounce every dysfunctional directional decree that I've declared over my life and I come in agreement that my life will

Now that you've come out of agreement with the words of the past, it's time to redirect your declarations. Here are some of the edits I made in my life that have been transformational in my journey to live the life I love:

Edit 1

Nobody likes me, everybody hates me, I even hate myself → → → **I love myself as God loves me. I am enough. I am worth being loved. Everyone doesn't have to like me but those that do are enriched by my life. I draw those around me who appreciate the gift I am and we make one another better people.**

Edit 2

I don't have the money →→→ **Finances, financial resources, and opportunities to generate revenue are presenting themselves to me to accomplish my goals. Where there are not finances, favor will show up.**

Edit 3

I'm not skinny enough to work in the entertainment industry or mainstream media→→→**People connect to my messages and not my size. My curves are beautiful and some viewers may be inspired to see my journey along the way.**

Edit 4

My dream is too big and too much→→→ **I am graced to carry a massive vision and the help I need to bring it to pass is on the way. I CAN do it all and have it all. I was graced to manage BIG things.**

Tell Those Lies... You've Changed

Now it's your turn!

It's time to fall out of agreement with dysfunction and into covenant with purpose. Think about the five biggest things you've said that have sent your life in a direction you never wanted it to go. Write them down and then edit them to redirect your future.

Edit 1

_____ →

_____

Edit 2

_____ →

_____

Edit 3

_____ →

_____

Edit 4

_____ →

_____

Moving Forward

Our words are creative and directional. I love the scripture that tells us to speak what is not as though it is. It's time to re-direct your life by redirecting your words. Like me, you may have had some directional declarations that you've sent out in the wrong direction, but it's never too late to resend them in a positive direction.

You have BIG dreams and you want to see them come to pass. Start making a conscious effort to send your words where you want to go in life.

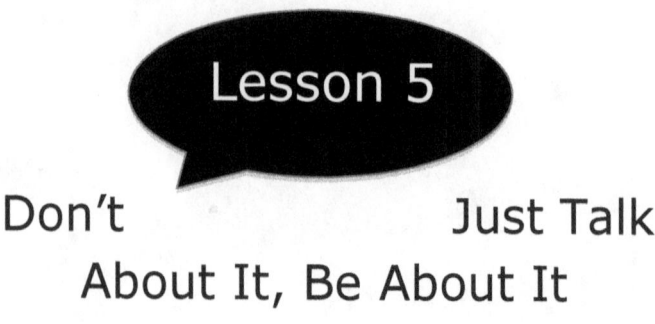

Don't Just Talk About It, Be About It

> Be the kind of person that when your feet hit the floor the Devil goes, "Awwww snap...They're up!"
>
> Daniela Gabrielle

Often times, people are afraid to make bold statements about their lives and the direction of their lives out of fear. Fear that it won't happen and then they'll be embarrassed.

Let's stop and deal with that for one moment!

It's not your responsibility to make your dream come true.

It's your responsibility to position yourself in the right place and take the steps of faith to move in that direction. You do your part and then you leave the rest up to God to show up and show out in your life.

Remember this, **your BIG dream is personal yet purposeful.** It's not about those sitting on the sidelines critiquing you; it's about you the one actually in the game. Think of it from the perspective of a professional athlete. There are millions of fans that tune in weekly to criticize or praise the performance of an athlete. Although their opinions may be outspoken and sometimes even disrespectful, the only person getting paid is the one playing the game.

Don't let the opinions of those watching from the sidelines distract you from your BIG dream. It's better to make a BIG declaration such as, I am going to start a business," start it, and fail than to say nothing and you end up internally tormented by a strong case of the "what-ifs."

Your bold declarations about what you are going to do in your life are said in public but they are not intended to benefit the public, they are intended to motivate you.

When you send your words out in the direction they should go, they will stir your faith and move you to action. Bold declarations hold **YOU** accountable for **YOUR** BIG dreams and make **YOU** move towards them. The reason so many people shy away from those directional declarations is because they are afraid they won't do it.

If you're going to be a person with a BIG mouth and BIG dreams, you have to determine in your heart, I am going to **DO** what I have been dreaming about. Your conversation is your first step of action. It is a reflection of your personal commitment.

At the beginning of year, I made a HUGE commitment to write ten books in one year. Not only did I make that commitment to myself, I strategically planned how I was going to make it happen. I then posted on my social media streams. If you stroll down my Facebook timeline and Twitter feed in December and January, you are bound to find videos and posts of me saying that I was going to write ten books in a year.

I encouraged people to help me push the books out by getting excited and not letting me forget the commitment I made. I didn't leave my commitment behind closed doors. I didn't make a decision to do something BIG and then disconnect from it.

My ten books in a year challenge stays before me on a daily basis. Between the reminders written on my mirrors and the Transitioners *(those are the community of goal-getters that gather with me on social media every day for inspiration, strategy, and motivation)* who won't let me forget what I said, I can't help but stay connected to that goal. I talk about writing these books on a consistent basis.

The more I hear myself say that I am writing ten books in one year, the more I desire to move in that direction. I find myself holding on to that promise of having a library full of books and resources written by me to pass down to my future generations.

If you're going to have a BIG mouth and BIG dreams, you are going to have to develop the mindset, agility and tenacity to back it up. Some of my favorite questions to ask clients is, "How bad do you want it? How bad do you want to see your BIG dream come true? How important is it for you to really see it manifest in your life? Is your dream non-negotiable?"

A non-negotiable dream is a dream that's not up for discussion. It's a dream, goal or promise you refuse to NOT pursue. Some things in our lives are good ideas. They are things that we would love to happen, but won't be hard pressed if they don't. Those are the ones that you'll compromise on and be okay if they don't quite work out.

It's okay to have those kinds of aspirations, but a non-negotiable dream will stick to you like glue. It's the calling that just doesn't go away. You think about it at night and you feel incomplete when you are not working on it.

Your non-negotiable dream is your passion. Within it you will discover your purpose on earth and that purpose is unshakable. Like you, I have an unshakable dream that's non-negotiable and no matter what I do, I can't get the vision of me accomplishing it out of my head. It's always there stirring inside of me even when all I want to do it forget about it.

We get like that because we know that the only person that can help us bring that BIG dream to life is God. At times, the responsibility of a non-negotiable dream can feel heavy, especially if we are trying to achieve them on our own. To avoid the added pressure of the world around us, we often settle to believe that it is much easier to keep our BIG dream to ourselves.

It's easy to get caught up in the hype of a silent dream. We can quickly believe the lies and forego what we were created to do and be. We've all been there. When I get to that place, I think about all of my favorite dreamers in the Bible who carried promises and saw them come to pass. My main man, Abraham, had a non-negotiable dream *(check out Genesis 12-21 for the full story)*. God promised him that He would make him a great nation and that he would multiply him greatly.

Abraham had a promise and dream of having an heir and leaving a legacy through his family line. No matter what Abraham went through, he could not shake that promise. It was non-negotiable and even in Abraham's errors, bad judgment calls and efforts to force feed results, the dream still came to pass.

One thing that I observed from Abraham's story is that God never stopped talking about the promise. He and Abraham were in constant conversation about the direction his life should be going. Often times, we stop talking about our dreams because we fear they won't happen. Like Abraham, in the midst of dream detours, that non-negotiable dream is still possible.

Don't let fear of failure stop you from taking action on your BIG dream. You have the dream in you for a reason. Be faithful to stick to it and be willing to realign yourself when you get off course. The only thing standing between you and your BIG dream is you and your willingness to keep moving. Continual movement and continual conversation towards the direction you want your life to go is critical in receiving your dream and promise.

As you begin sending your words in the direction you want them to go it's vital to transform your conversation. Don't just talk about your BIG dreams, be about your BIG dreams. Stop talking about what you are going to do and start talking about what you **ARE** doing.

Update your declarations from "I am going to", to "I am." "I am going to" is a declaration of intent, but "I am" is a declaration of activity. It means that you are actively moving in the direction you want your life to go.

Let's take a look at a pop culture example of a woman that lived in intent. To know me is to know that I love a good unscripted reality TV show. They get a pretty bad reputation, kind of like the mouth does, but I have picked up some really interesting life lessons watching other people's lives unfold on my television screen.

A popular reality TV show is The Real Housewives of Atlanta and a few seasons ago, they had a cast member that started with the show from the beginning. Each season, they followed her as she talked about what she was "going to do." She was going to start a clothing line and she was going to build a house. For multiple seasons we saw her intent, but we never experienced her activity. Eventually, it caused her reign on reality television to collapse. What a major waste of a platform, all because her actions did not line up with her words.

Good intent doesn't bring dreams to fruition, action does. Transform your declarations to drive your actions and start declaring what you ARE doing until you start doing it. Tell yourself over and over what you ARE doing and then do it. Your directional declarations will undergird your action and hold you accountable to what you desire to do.

In order to align your words and send them in the direction that you want your life to go, get clear about where you see your life heading. There's a quote from an unknown author that says, **"If you don't have a plan for your life, someone else will."** It's the same for our words. If we don't have a plan for our words, something that we are targeting our faith towards, we'll spend our conversations talking recklessly and idly.

READY. AIM. FIRE.

Say this out loud right now,

"I have a BIG plan for my words. My words will cause me to propel & prosper."

Your Big Dream Directional Declaration

It's time to talk your life in the direction you want to see it move. Start by brainstorming where you want to see your life in ten years.

In ten years, I see myself...

_____
_____
_____
_____
_____
_____
_____
_____
_____
_____
_____
_____
_____
_____
_____

BIG MOUTH BIG DREAMS

To achieve your ten-year plan, it's important to identify milestone goals that will get you where you need to be. Think about the top ten power moves that will bring you exactly where you need to be.

1) _____

2) _____

3) _____

4) _____

5) _____

6) _____

7) _____

8) _____

9) _____

10) _____

Once you know where you want to go and what you need to do to get there, it's time to identify things that you need to make it happen. It may be discipline, finances, resources, a babysitter, a trainer or somewhere in between. Write down the top ten things that you need physically, emotionally, spiritually and financially to get to the life you see for yourself in ten years.

Get creative and think **BIG**!

1) _____

2) _____

3) _____

4) _____

5) _____

6) _____

7) _____

8) _____

9) _____

10) _____

Now that you are clear on your plan, it's time to send your words in this direction. Write bold one-sentence declarations that you can infuse into your daily conversations.

1) _____

_____

_____

2) _____

_____

_____

3) _____

_____

_____

4) _____

_____

_____

5)_____

_____

_____

6)_____

_____

_____

7)_____

_____

_____

8)_____

_____

_____

BIG MOUTH BIG DREAMS

9) _____

_____

_____

10) _____

_____

Lesson 6

Say What You Want and Want What You Say

> Delight thyself also in the Lord: and he shall give thee the desires of thine heart.
>
> Psalms 37:4 KJV

Getting to your BIG dream takes heart, a whole lot of gut busting, mountain moving, get knocked down but I get up again never giving up heart! You were equipped with that heart along with the necessary tools to get your BIG dream in motion. Everything that you need is in you, if you'll get out of your own way. The only thing standing between you and your BIG dream is you.

You have to find the courage to stand firm in your aspirations and let nothing sway your conversation or actions from moving in the direction you really want your life to go.

As I told you when we started this journey, I had a BIG mouth. I was loud, I was opinionated and I talked a mile a minute, however, my BIG mouth was not bringing me anywhere closer to where I wanted to be. Being a BIG mouth isn't an automatic pass to reaching your goals. It's a tool used to enhance or hinder you from purpose and destiny.

Here I was with all the words in the world, but I never took the time to form my mouth to admit what was really important for my life. I never stopped to set my boundaries when people ran over every area of my life.

I refused to speak up when I was unhappy with the terrible hairstyle I got at the beauty salon. There was no way I was even going to dream of telling anyone that I had a dream of owning a multi-billion dollar entertainment conglomerate that helped others birth their big dreams and take them to market using media and pop culture. To imagine me fessing up to wanting to live a jet setters life as an opposed to the traditional life my friends and family led was completely out of the picture. Since I didn't have the guts to say it, I definitely lacked the confidence to pursue it; therefore my life was just as lack luster as my BIG mouth.

It's Time to Crack the Code on Your Mouth

You've got a BIG dream and it's time to activate your faith by saying what you want. I don't mean saying what is politically correct, socially acceptable and family approved. It's time to say what you really want until you see it in your life. Don't stop talking about it until it manifests no matter who agrees or disagrees.

The moment I got honest with myself about what I really wanted out of life, from the little things to the big things, I was able to articulate them. Once I started articulating them, I started seeing them pop up all around me. Some things came quickly and others took awhile, but it started by breaking my silence about what I wanted for me.

You cannot continue to be apologetic for what you want. If you want your meat prepared medium well, ask for it. If you want the five-bedroom home with the deck and pool, look for it. It you want to start a business in China, start preparing yourself for what you want. Every time you have a true desire that you know is pure and honest, open up your mouth and say what you want.

READY. AIM. FIRE.

Say this out loud right now,

"I won't apologize for what I want!"

I can remember the day I finally got the guts to say that I wanted to quit my job, move to Florida and plant my business headquarters. It took me actually verbalizing that desire for me to grasp and accept that plan for my life. It was untraditional, it was risky, but most of all it was what I wanted. Once I started saying I wanted to move to Florida, it woke up my senses to everything started moving in the right direction.

Think about it, it's not until you start saying that you want a white-on-white BMW with the sunroof that you start seeing them. Then all of the sudden everywhere you go, you see that car or a car like it. It's not that the car never existed, it's that until you spoke it out of your mouth you weren't aware of how attainable what you want really was.

Stop lying to yourself about the life that you want and start saying what you want. Of course there is a catch to this. You cannot say what you want and not accept responsibility for what comes along with that desire. If you say you want that house, then you have to also be willing to accept the mortgage that comes along with it.

Every BIG dream will come at a price. Let's go back to my favorite life-planning tool, the Bible, where Jesus is dropping some major knowledge that applies to our BIG dream situations.

For which of you, intending to build a tower, sitteth not down first, and counteth the cost, whether he have sufficient to finish it?

Luke 14:28

You're building your BIG dream with your BIG mouth, but it's like my momma used to say, "Make sure your mouth don't write a check your behind can't cash." This doesn't mean that you abandon your BIG dream because you don't have the capital necessary to make it happen right now. It simply means that you have thought about what comes along with your BIG dream and you are willing to pay the cost for it.

Build your dream with intent. Build it on purpose with purpose. As you reach towards it think about all the good and bad that come with it and prepare your heart to accept it.

It amazes me the amount of celebrities end up broke and broken because they didn't fully count the cost of fame. Sure, they put the hard work in to get there, but did they consider the effects of being in the limelight? Did they factor into their BIG dream that going to the grocery store or Wal-mart will never be the same?

We have to be authentic about what we want and trust that when it gets here, God will give us the grace to handle it. For years and years, I spent my time dreaming, praying, and boldly declaring that I was going to have a successful business that paid for my lifestyle. I believed that I would be on television and on the road doing what I do best, empowering and training others. I spent years crying out to God for this promise. I invested countess hours and dollars funding this dream. I went to school to be better prepared. I was fully committed to the dream and then it happened, the call to appear on my first television talk show and my first event hosted by me in my newfound company headquarters.

After all of that talking about what I wanted, it was here and where was I? Hiding under the covers in my bed saying, "I'm not ready!"

Fear came to grip me and keep me from walking into the very thing I asked God to give me. I had to get real and ask myself, "You said what you wanted Daniela and now it's here, did you REALLY want what you said?" Well of course, I wanted it. It was here and if I wanted it, I had to take the territory that came with it. I had to press past fear, nervousness, and personal insecurities because this was what I wanted. It was time to get out of that bed and get to my BIG dream.

I had to give myself several pep talks to get from under those covers, but I did it. I reminded myself of exactly who I was and what I was created to do. One of the advantages of being a BIG mouth is that you are the first partaker of the fruit of your words. When you are feeling down, insecure, or inadequate for your BIG dream, you have the ability to speak yourself out of that pity party and into a promise party.

I threw myself a promise party by reminding myself of every BIG dream and BIG promise that I was standing on in my life. I kept reinforcing those promises with my words and each time I got nervous I reminded myself that this was my promise coming to pass.

I went forward with my event and my TV appearance. As a result I gained new clients, expanded my brand, and created a new video reel that I would never have without moving forward. I had more to gain by moving forward than standing still. Once you decide that you want your BIG dream more than you want to be comfortable, you'll hear yourself pipe up and use that BIG mouth to talk you into your BIG dreams.

Your BIG Dream Want List

Now that you've been empowered, it's time to say what you what. Take some time to reflect on what you really want out of life. Write them in this declaration and read them aloud each day. Stick close to these wants and date them as they come to pass.

I want _____ Date _____

I want _____ Date _____

I want _____ Date _____

I want _____ Date _____

I want _____ Date _____

I want _____ Date _____

I want _____ Date _____

I want _____ Date _____

I want _____ Date _____

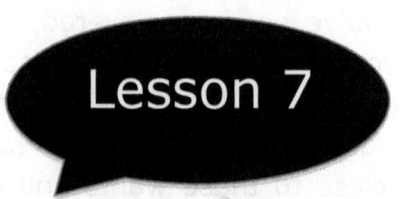

Lesson 7

~~It Is What It Is~~, Correction, It Is What I Declare

> "God has already done everything He's going to do. The ball is now in your court. If you want success, if you want wisdom, if you want to be prosperous and healthy, you're going to have to do more than meditate and believe; you must boldly declare words of faith and victory over yourself and your family."

Once I came into the knowledge that the power of life and death is in what came out of my BIG mouth, it was time for me to starting slinging my words in new directions. There are many types of communication that our BIG mouths are capable of. We can have conversations, we can give ourselves those pep talks that we talked about earlier, and we can release words into our atmosphere that transform our lives and the lives around us.

One of the most powerful and pin-pointing exercises of your faith and BIG mouth are declarations and decrees. Although similar, they are not completely one in the same. A declaration is a positive, explicit, or formal statement made to announce the state of a thing. In American history, one of the most famous declarations written was the Declaration of Independence drafted by Thomas Jefferson between June 11 and June 28 of 1776. This declaration announced that the thirteen newly independent sovereign states were no longer a part of the British Empire. This declaration forever changed both American and British history.

Just as these bold colonies made an announcement that life would no longer look like it was, there is a need in your life to break away. Do something bold and be BIG enough to make an announcement about it. When you release declarations over your life, what you are saying is that life as you've known it in a particular area has changed. You send notice to everything and everyone around you.

Often in life, when we are ready to experience change or are in the process of making a change, we keep it secret. We often don't take our life changes to the public, out of fear of retribution.

What if what we change doesn't work? When you make a declaration over your life, you cut ties with the past. Everything around you has to come in line with the change. It's not always easy, but it will happen.

It's no secret that Daniela Gabrielle is not my birth name. I spent the first thirty years of my life going by the name that my mother and father named me until one day, I realized that it was time for a radical change in my life. It wasn't a mid-life crisis or the exit from the twenties talking, it was God pouring into me visions of a life I couldn't even imagine.

It was so far from anything I had ever seen for my life. I was going to be a completely different woman, with a completely different life. I wouldn't do the same thing, go the same places, or be connected to the former things.

The story of transforming my life and changing my name was a lot like the passage in the Bible where God was talking to the children of Israel and He told them that world would see His righteousness through them *(it's a an inspiring story about redefining, check it out in Isaiah 62).*

In the midst of that he declared to them that he would name them with a new name. This was God redefining who they were and how they would impact the world. That's what was happening to me. My life was being redefined and each time that people called me by my new name they called me into my purpose on the earth.

Now, a name change for many is much too drastic of a move and honestly, I don't recommend it unless there is a huge conviction in your heart to do it. I share the story with you because it was a change that I had to make. When I decided that I would agree with God, concerning His new plan for my life and I accepted the new name, I had to make a decision as to what came next. I could have kept the experience to myself and allowed it to be an internal change or I could begin to declare this newfound name and lifestyle.

I chose to declare that I had a new name and a new vision. I made a public announcement about being Daniela Gabrielle. Living in the age of technology, I took to Facebook where I addressed the name change and life change in a note that remained on my page for about a year to help people recognize and understand the transition. The more I declared that I was Daniela Gabrielle, the more my life began to line up with my declaration. I declared over my life every promise that came along with my change. I stood on the promises that accompanied change. I held strong to my profession of faith and I haven't let go.

There were a few things I learned in that process about declarations. Declarations are public, but as public as they are, a declaration influences you. The more you hear yourself declare God's promises over your life the more you'll believe what you say. With each declaration your faith will rise and your actions will begin to align. Every time I declared that I was Daniela Gabrielle, my life moved in that direction. Declarations are directional. They will move you in the direction you want to go.

Think about where you whole-heartedly want your life to go. Declare what "will be" as "what is" right now. Don't wait until you see it to say it, start saying it in present tense.

For example, if you are holding on to a promise that you will have a child, declare that your womb is open and fertile to receive it's seed. If you believe for a promotion, declare that the doors of promotion are open for you and that the right opportunity is presenting itself in your life. If you are in school, declare that that the career you want will be waiting on the other side.

BIG Mouth Activation

Be bold about what it is that you are declaring over your life and your family. It's time to make an announcement about who you are and what you believe to be "truth" for *your* life. Write down what you declare for these areas of your life and spend time daily speaking these declarations out loud.

My BIG Dream Declaration

I declare that _____

_____

_____

My BIG Family Declaration

I declare that _____

_____

_____

My BIG Spiritual Walk Declaration

I declare that _____

_____

_____

My BIG Health & Wellness Declaration

I declare that _____

_____

_____

My BIG Career Declaration

I declare that _____

_____

_____

My BIG Education Declaration

I declare that _____

_____

_____

My BIG Wealth & Finance Declaration

I declare that _____

_____

_____

My BIG Year Declaration (20__)

I declare that _____

_____

_____

My BIG _____ Declaration

I declare that _____

_____

_____

My BIG _____ Declaration

I declare that I declare that _____

_____

_____

Lesson 8

You Are Destined For The Finish

> "Being confident of this very thing, that he which hath begun a good work in you will perform it until the day of Jesus Christ"
>
> Philippians 1:6

As I have shared some of the most powerful lessons that I have experienced about using my BIG mouth to speak my BIG dreams into existence, you should see your own BIG dreams starting to get bigger and your BIG mouth starting to confess some new and positive things to help you get there. Your faith should be stirred and ignited for the next level of your life. So the question now becomes, what in the world do I do next?

Now what? After all of the BIG talk and the BIG

dreams, you are going to have to put in some BIG investments. Let your words move you to a place of action. Don't be overwhelmed by what is before you. Keep in mind that when it comes to your BIG dream that you're not doing it alone. It's your job to accept the BIG dream and walk out the steps that you feel led to walk in your heart. You have to be willing to trust God with what you cannot control.

With every BIG step that you take, keep this in mind; **you were destined for the finish**. I love that word destined. It sounds so official. You were bound for a certain destination and that destination is the finish line. Each year you set goals for your life and whether you got there or not in the past, this year it's time to tell yourself, ***"I will finish what I started."***

READY. AIM. FIRE.

Say this out loud right now,

"I am destined for the finish!"

Don't abandon your BIG dream, being moved by what you see or are currently experiencing. Stay faithful to what you believe in your life and tailor your conversation for the finish. To finish is to bring to an end or to completion. You have everything you need inside of you to bring your BIG dream to completion.

A BIG dream is merely the big picture to many smaller goals or what I like to call BIG dream milestones. It took me ninety days to discover, write out, and craft an action plan to reach my BIG dream. I actually have a pretty large printed binder that holds the promises of my BIG dream and I use it as a roadmap to change. This is something I teach in my audio coaching and workbook series, "Inaugurate Your Life."

To ensure that I'm always diligently working towards the big picture, I set a vision that aligns with my BIG dream for each year. Then I break down my vision into quarterly and monthly milestones that align with my BIG dream. Each day I act on my milestones is a day I'm actively living my BIG dream.

If you're going to live in your BIG dream, you have to start by tailoring your conversation for the finish. Like we talked about earlier, shift your conversation from "I will" to "I am."

Like I did with my own personal BIG dream milestones, determine what you are doing in this year and in this month for that matter. Once you determine what you are doing and visualize yourself doing it, agree with God that you are willing to take the steps of faith that it will take to make it happen. Then start talking about the direction you are going.

What are you doing to live your BIG dream this year?

The most effective way to activate your BIG Mouth Big Dream Year is to stand at the end of your year and visualize what you have accomplished. Once you can see your desired end, work backwards to create a realistic plan to get to the finish line. Break that vision up into four quarterly milestones with monthly action steps.

This Year's BIG Dream Vision

Quarter 1 Milestone	
Month	Action Items
#1	
#2	
#3	
Quarter 2 Milestone	
Month	Action Items
#1	
#2	
#3	

Quarter 3 Milestone	
Month	Action Items
#1	
#2	
#3	
Quarter 4 Milestone	
#1	
#2	
#3	

BIG MOUTH BIG DREAMS

Your BIG dream is your vision for purpose and destiny. You have to be married to the vision and not the process or you will be heartbroken each time life derails you. Keep focused on the BIG dream ahead and don't let go.

In tough times, remind yourself that you are destined for the finish. Keep the picture of your finish line at the front of your mind on a regular basis.

Now that you've solved the problem of what to do next, the other burning issue concerning getting to the finish is having the character necessary to remain at the place you desire to go. There's a common quote that says,

"Your gift can take you somewhere your character can't keep you." In essence, this is having the appropriate character to maintain your BIG dream.

For example, you may be the person desiring to lose a large amount of weight. You've written out your dream to be a size XYZ, you've been boldly declaring that your losing weight,, and you've even started working out, however you struggle with discipline. Discipline is a major character strength needed to get to the finish in this situation.

You get to the finish with character confessions. Begin to let your BIG mouth lead you to good character and disciplined habits. Create the characteristics necessary to maintain the next level of your dream by speaking what's not as though they were. Start identifying what characteristics you need to get where you're going and begin confessing them about yourself.

I am a very creative person and with creativity come a lot of randomness and disorganization. I personally battle because the businesswoman and my creativity often war within me. If I was going to take my business to the next level and become the CEO I desired to be, it required me to shift from merely being a creative professional to being a business leader.

In the beginning I was lacking the structure and discipline needed to succeed. I could've given in and said, I'm just a creative personality; this BIG dream of running multiple companies isn't for me. Instead, I chose to transform who I was in business by releasing character confessions about the mogul I wanted to be. I identified what made great moguls in business and I began to confess that I possessed those characteristics.

I said them until I became them. I found outlets and resources to be what I needed to be without denying who I truly was. Now, my creativity runs in unity with my inner mogul. They work together to make me good at what I do.

What characteristics are critical to getting you to your finish line?

1. _____
2. _____
3. _____
4. _____
5. _____

Here's the good news! The finish line is calling you towards your BIG dream. Open your BIG mouth and let it start talking you into the life of your dreams. Don't hold back in any area. It's time to put your BIG mouth to use. Use it for good. Use it for purpose. Use it to unlock your BIG dream.

BIG MOUTH BIG DREAMS

Part II

The Dreamer's Charge

BIG MOUTH BIG DREAMS

The Dreamer's Charge

A charge is an authoritative directive set to stir, empower and set a strategic mission in motion. It comes with power and strength. As you read this charge, may your BIG dream be set in motion and your BIG mouth set in order.

Read this charge over and over. Let it seep into every fiber of your being. Let it move you to action. Let it unlock what you were created to do and be. This is my charge to you.

Today I declare that you are enough. Your ideas are enough. Your dream is enough. Your personality is enough. You will not shrink back from being the amazing person you are. I speak to your heart and declare that you are FREE. You are free to be and do all that God placed in your heart. Your life matters and you so do your BIG dreams.

I charge you to boldly declare what is for your life. Speak those things that are not as though they were. Say what is important and ask for what you need. You will not come up short on the road to your destiny. Everything that you need is wrapped up in your words. I charge you to unlock your potential with positive confessions.

You have fought for everyone and everything else. Today I fight for you. I declare that nothing will stop you from speaking life to your situations. I speak favor over your footsteps and faith over your vocabulary. Let your heart overflow with positive confessions of who you are and what you will become. Let every word of negativity and destruction be uprooted from your heart and detached from your memory. You are NOT who they said you were and you will not be what they said you would be. You are greater and you will do greater.

Agree with God that you are favored and blessed. Accept the grace that is extended through His love. I charge you to walk the walk and talk the talk simultaneously, and I decree that where you falter, He will be your strength. Break out from that downtrodden place. Rise up and build the life of your dreams. You deserve it and it deserves you.

Today marks a new chapter in your life. I declare that you will never ever be the same. May you encounter abundance, joy, love, and peace every day. May your words deliver those very things to the world around you. This is your time...Speak your BIG dream into existence.

BIG MOUTH BIG DREAMS

Part III

21- Days of Big Mouthed Dream Activation

BIG MOUTH BIG DREAMS

Dear BIG Dreamer,

You've read the lessons and received your charge, now the real journey begins. This is where you take what you've learned and use it to transform your conversation. There's nothing in life worse than unutilized information. As you've grown to love and accept your BIG dream, it's time to fill your mouth with those words. Research shows that it takes twenty-one days to create a habit. Over the next twenty-one days, activate your BIG dream vocabulary by reading these compilations of affirmations, declarations, confessions and decrees aloud three times a day. As you read it, meditate on its content and record your thoughts in the activation diary.

This is your time. Ready. Aim. Activate.

I love you to life,

Daniela Gabrielle

BIG MOUTH BIG DREAMS

Ready. Aim. Activate.

Day One: I Declare Victory

....

I believe that I am victorious, even when victory is not visible in my life. I trust that all things work together for my good. My setback is a setup for something that I cannot imagine right now. I choose to agree that God knows what is best for my life and I declare that this alternate route is bringing me to a better place than where I started. This is my journey and I will not be deterred.

....

ACTIVATION DIARY

_____
_____
_____
_____
_____
_____
_____

BIG MOUTH BIG DREAMS

Ready. Aim. Activate.

Day Two: It's So Amazing

....

God can amaze me with something far greater than I originally imagined. My plans are unfolding perfectly, day by day. My dream is opening up and expanding by the minute and I have the tools, resources and stamina to experience them in their fullness. My BIG dream overflows.

....

ACTIVATION DIARY

_____
_____
_____
_____

_____
_____
_____

BIG MOUTH BIG DREAMS

Ready. Aim. Activate.

Day Three: There's Room For Me

....

My gifts are making room for me in the marketplace, in business, in the community, & in the world around me. I will rise up & use what's in me to radically transform my faith, my finances ,& my sphere of influence! I will empower & influence those around me to be the best version of them. I don't leave my gifts & talents at home. I take them everywhere I go & they cause me to prosper.

....

ACTIVATION DIARY

_____
_____
_____
_____

BIG MOUTH BIG DREAMS

DANIELA GABRIELLE

Ready. Aim. Activate.

Day Four: And Still I Thrive

....

I do not exist, I THRIVE. My life is increasing! My joy is increasing! My paychecks are increasing! My abilities are increasing! My platform is increasing! My faith that God can & will do exceeding abundant above all that I can think or imagine is increasing! This is the season my dream will MANIFEST. My voice will be heard, my face will be seen, but most of all God's plan for my life will be experienced. I lack nothing & am grateful for everything.

....

ACTIVATION DIARY

_____
_____
_____
_____
_____
_____
_____

BIG MOUTH BIG DREAMS

Ready. Aim. Activate.

Day Five: The Sound of Abundance

....

Abundance isn't my wish, abundance is my birthright! I am an heir to overflow & today I walk in my "more than enough" lifestyle. I am more than enough, my resources are more than enough, my finances are more than enough, my gifts are more than enough, & my relationships are more than enough. Lack no longer knows my name. I am chased down by opportunity & overtaken by wealth & favor. Everywhere I look, I see overflow. Every time I listen, I hear abundance. Every place I go, I have more than enough.

....

ACTIVATION DIARY

_____

_____

BIG MOUTH BIG DREAMS

Ready. Aim. Activate.

Day Six: Extra! Extra! Read All About It

....

The favor, finances, resources, & wisdom I need to achieve my EXTRAORDINARY dream is within reach. I am bold enough to DO, wise enough to ASK, & crazy enough to GO where others have not to experience the life I love. There are no limits to what I can do, have, or experience. An EXTRAORDINARY life is achievable & I'm worthy of the EXTRA investment.

....

ACTIVATION DIARY

_____
_____
_____
_____

BIG MOUTH BIG DREAMS

Ready. Aim. Activate.

Day Seven: Down With Discouragement

....

I will not let the voices of discouragement keep me from moving forward. I'm about to see a return on my investment! Every sacrifice I make for my dream is yielding a return. I don't quit and I won't quit. I refuse to believe lies! The end of this story is victory! I celebrate my BIG turn around & even BIGGER breakthrough.

....

ACTIVATION DIARY

_____
_____
_____
_____
_____
_____
_____

BIG MOUTH BIG DREAMS

Ready. Aim. Activate.

Day Eight: Can't Stop My Flow

....

If God is for me, who can stand against me? Opposition merely puts pressure on my creativity so that I can recognize just how gifted I am. I don't run, I press through! I let my potential rise to the top and I continually learn that I am greater than I think!

....

ACTIVATION DIARY

_____
_____
_____
_____
_____
_____
_____
_____
_____
_____

BIG MOUTH BIG DREAMS

Ready. Aim. Activate.

Day Nine: Fall In Line

....

I have what it takes to experience my BIG dream. I can handle it. I can achieve it. I attract everything I need to bring that vision forth. My character is in alignment. My vocabulary is in alignment. My will is in alignment. My finances and resources are in alignment. My BIG dream is within reach and I live in my BIG dream in every capacity.

....

ACTIVATION DIARY

_____
_____
_____
_____
_____
_____
_____

BIG MOUTH BIG DREAMS

Ready. Aim. Activate.

Day Ten: Hanging Out In The Deep

....

I am comfortable being uncomfortable and willing to push through the unknown to do business in the deep. Fear does not rule me; nor does it dictate my direction. I live in deep waters. The deep is where BIG stuff happens. I have a front seat ticket to miracles in my life. I will not miss my season or be late for divine appointments. I will arrive to destiny on time and in one piece. God WILL finish what He started in me.

....

ACTIVATION DIARY

_____
_____
_____
_____

BIG MOUTH BIG DREAMS

Ready. Aim. Activate.

Day Eleven: Moving Forward

....

I refuse to let people who are doing nothing, sit back and tell me what I cannot do. My life is limitless and expansive. I declare that the mouths of the naysayers have no impact on my movement. My BIG dreams are moving. My life is moving. My career is moving. My family is moving. My finances are moving. My vision is moving. I was born for a time as this and no matter what is said, I declare that I keep moving forward!

....

ACTIVATION DIARY

_____
_____
_____
_____

BIG MOUTH BIG DREAMS

Ready. Aim. Activate.

Day Twelve: Accelerated Expansion

....

This is my year of ACCELERATED EXPANSION. I not only experience vertical growth but I also experience exhaustive lateral growth that creates multiple streams of prosperity in my life. My BIG dream is moving at an accelerated pace. Time that was wasted or lost is being made up in this season. My life is growing into something far greater than I ever expected.

....

ACTIVATION DIARY

_____
_____
_____
_____
_____
_____
_____
_____

BIG MOUTH BIG DREAMS

Ready. Aim. Activate.

Day Thirteen: A Gift To The World

....

I am a gift to the world. I was created to change nations, influence cultures, & breathe life where there is no hope. I will not deny the world of the "gift of me." I will freely give of myself in abundance. I will make the world around me a better place by simply being me. I am needed and necessary. My voice is filled with words of comfort, peace and wisdom. I share them freely wherever I go.

....

ACTIVATION DIARY

_____
_____
_____
_____

BIG MOUTH BIG DREAMS

Ready. Aim. Activate.

Day Fourteen: Perfect Timing

....

This is the perfect time for me to believe God for the impossible, experience the incredible, walk in the indescribable, & receive the immeasurable. My life runs over with solutions and answers.

....

ACTIVATION DIARY

_____
_____
_____
_____
_____
_____
_____
_____
_____

BIG MOUTH BIG DREAMS

Ready. Aim. Activate.

Day Fifteen: Just One Step Away

I am just one step away from breaking through to my next level. It only takes one phone call, one meeting, one introduction, or one act of faith to topple into my new place. My eyes are open, my ears are on high alert and my heart is sensitive to the opportunities that will transform my BIG dream. I will take my next step even if it's scary. I will ask the hard questions and do what hasn't been done before. I declare that the windows of Heaven are open and as I take a step forward, favor will meet me there.

ACTIVATION DIARY

_____
_____
_____
_____

BIG MOUTH BIG DREAMS

Ready. Aim. Activate.

Day Sixteen: Nothing Stands Between Me & My Breakthrough

I am unbreakable, unstoppable, and uncontainable. I overflow with the power of God living in me. With Him I cannot fail. Failure is not an option, because it's not my portion. I am engrafted into the inheritance of the King. He has provided the strength and grace I need to succeed. Nothing stands between me and my Big dream that I can't overcome.

ACTIVATION DIARY

_____
_____
_____
_____

BIG MOUTH BIG DREAMS

Ready. Aim. Activate.

Day Seventeen: Unlock The Wealth Within

I may not have been born with a silver spoon in my mouth, but I was definitely born with solutions in my heart. What I need to succeed is IN me! I have both the capability and capacity to solve the problems in my life. Solutions to my situations are manifesting and they are unlocking my wealth from within.

ACTIVATION DIARY

_____
_____
_____
_____

_____
_____
_____

BIG MOUTH BIG DREAMS

Ready. Aim. Activate.

Day Eighteen: I Am Not Afraid

....

Greatness is my portion & abundance is my destiny. I refuse to settle for less than my full potential. I have great potential and I live up to it. I give God permission to raise the bar in my life and I respond by stepping up to the challenge. I choose not to settle for mediocrity even in the face of adversity. I don't apologize for the greatness in me. My standards are high and my rewards are even higher. I am not afraid of my BIG dream. I embrace it and live it everyday.

....

ACTIVATION DIARY

_____
_____
_____

BIG MOUTH BIG DREAMS

Ready. Aim. Activate.

Day Nineteen: The Ultimate Refusal

....

I refuse to be a slave to the fear of failure. Mistakes are a natural part of transition. I will not allow the fear of failure to keep me from moving towards my BIG dream. I move in confidence and boldness. I believe that every step propels me forward. The decision I make NOW directly impacts my future. I choose wisely and trust that any move is better than no move at all. Even my perceived failures are setting me up for a favorable future.

....

ACTIVATION DIARY

_____
_____
_____
_____

BIG MOUTH BIG DREAMS

Ready. Aim. Activate.

Day Twenty: To The Top

It's not a matter of **CAN I**, it's matter of **WILL I** and **YES, I WILL**. I will go all the way to the top! The top of my game, top of my class, top of my industry, and the top of my potential! I will go there because I declare that I am willing to do what others are not, to have what others don't have. The top is where I belong. I am comfortable there, because I was born to be there. I am destined to live on the top.

ACTIVATION DIARY

_____
_____
_____
_____

BIG MOUTH BIG DREAMS

DANIELA GABRIELLE

Ready. Aim. Activate.

Day Twenty-One: I Want It All

I WANT IT ALL! It's not a reflection of greed but an echo of God's heart for my life. I will not apologize for my BIG dream, and I am not sorry for perusing my desires. I am okay with living life full on. I'm willing to accept what comes with my BIG dream. I am well equipped to handle what God has placed in my stewardship. I will not ruin what has been given to me. Everything that I touch will prosper.

ACTIVATION DIARY

_____
_____
_____
_____

BIG MOUTH BIG DREAMS

ABOUT THE AUTHOR

Daniela Gabrielle, The Transition Entrepreneur is a bestselling author and motivational speaker. As the CEO of Motique Momentums, LLC and it's seven subsidiaries she has embraced the role of a serial entrepreneur, empowering others as a transition coach, business and branding consultant, and media personality.

This media mogul chose to transform her life from ordinary to extraordinary by abandoning her comfortable surroundings to go after the life and career she always dreamed of. She has coined the phrase, "Live the Life You Love" and uses this matra to help people across the globe change, transition, and emerge.

For Booking Inquiries e-mail:
info@danielaGabrielle.com

Stay Connected!
www.danielaGabrielle.com
www.facebook.com/chatDaniG
wwww.twitter.com/chatDaniG

DANIELA GABRIELLE

The program will guide you through writing, self-publishing, marketing and executing your first book launch. This hands on program includes:

- (8) Group Coaching Sessions to guide you through your book writing process
- (4-6) One on One Coaching/Consulting Sessions to develop your marketing strategy and book launch event
- Cover Art designed by Motique Momentums
- Manuscript Formatting by MOTIQUE Media
- Forward or endorsement written by Daniela Gabrielle
- Bio and sales copy for the back of the book written by MOTIQUE Media
- Featured in Limitless Living Online Magazine
- Access to Daniela Gabrielle via e-mail for advice during the duration of the program
- Lifetime Aspiring Authors Association Membership which provides discounts on seminars, courses and conferences

www.danielaGabrielle.com

HAPPY
DREAMING!

www.ingramcontent.com/pod-product-compliance
Lightning Source LLC
Chambersburg PA
CBHW070156100426
42743CB00013B/2926